J
743
Joh
Johnson
Let's celebrate St. Patrick's
Day

R440474
9.65

# Let's Celebrate
# St. Patrick's Day
## A Book of Drawing Fun

Written and Illustrated by
**Pamela Johnson**

**Watermill Press**

# Introduction

*Cead mile failte!* That's Gaelic for "A hundred thousand welcomes!" This greeting, in the old Irish tongue, can be heard on St. Patrick's Day!

In the Irish countryside, March 17th is a day for visiting friends and relatives. There are songs, and concerts, and plays about St. Patrick, Ireland's patron saint. There's even a big parade in his honor—and everybody wears green! For "the wearin' of the green" is a symbol of springtime and the green grass of Ireland.

You can draw the symbols of St. Patrick's Day. It's easy! And it's fun! Each of the drawings in this book is shown in several simple steps. Just follow each step, adding to your drawing as you go along. Soon you'll have your own St. Patrick's Day friends to help you celebrate the holiday!

Are you ready to begin?

Let's go to the Emerald Isle!

IRELAND

# Materials

You'll need paper, pencils, and an eraser to start. When your drawing looks the way you want it to, color it with crayons, colored markers, or water-color paints.

Remember, the best part of your drawing is what *you* add to it with a little imagination. Don't be afraid to experiment! And, most of all, have fun!

# The Irish Country Cottage

Green stands for nature! Green stands for hope! Green stands for Ireland! Covered with the greenest of valleys and fields, Ireland is known as The Emerald Isle. The countryside is dotted with bright white cottages, old stone walls, ruined castles, and churches.

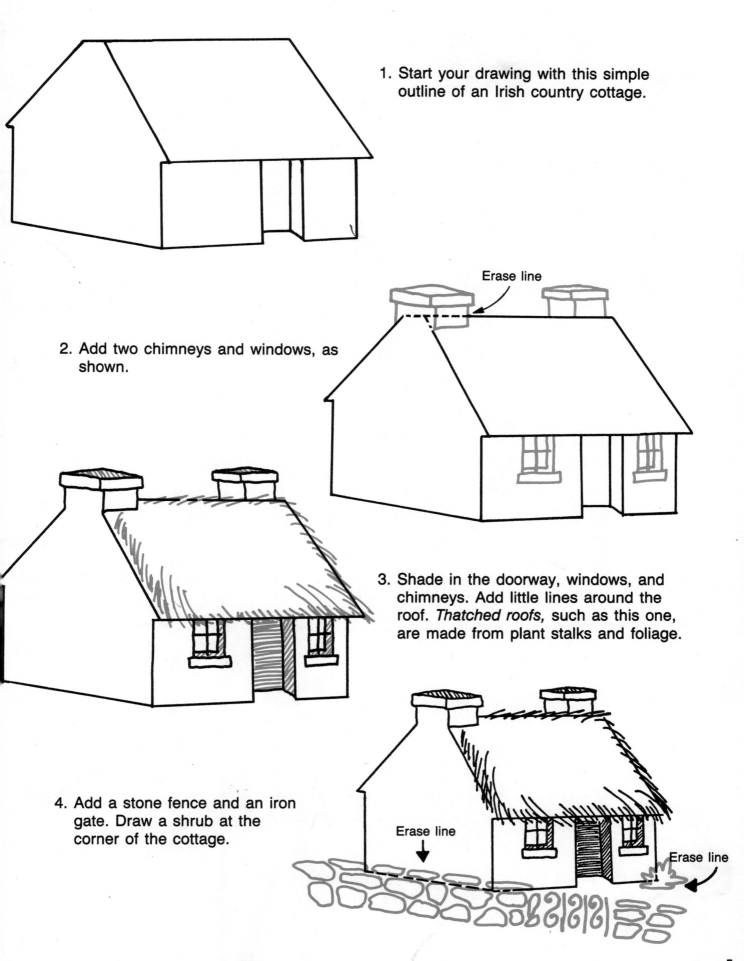

1. Start your drawing with this simple outline of an Irish country cottage.

2. Add two chimneys and windows, as shown.

Erase line

3. Shade in the doorway, windows, and chimneys. Add little lines around the roof. *Thatched roofs,* such as this one, are made from plant stalks and foliage.

4. Add a stone fence and an iron gate. Draw a shrub at the corner of the cottage.

Erase line

Erase line

# Leprechauns

In Irish folklore, the leprechaun is a sprightly elf and a trickster. If you capture one, don't let him go—he might lead you to his pot o' gold!

Turn the page for more holiday fun!

1. Start with an oval for the body, and a circle for the head. Add the beginnings of the arms, legs, and hand. Draw the leprechaun's pipe, as shown.

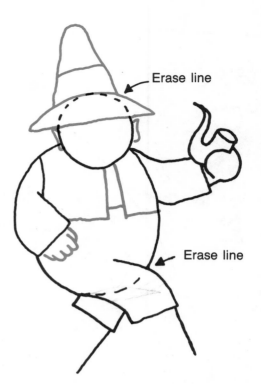

Erase line

Erase line

2. Add the ears and hat. Add the vest and shirt. Now fill in the other hand.

3. Add details to the clothes. Now complete the legs. Add long, pointy shoes, as shown.

4. Fill in the leprechaun's mischievous face. Draw fingers on his hand. Add his coattails, flapping in the breeze.

Erase line

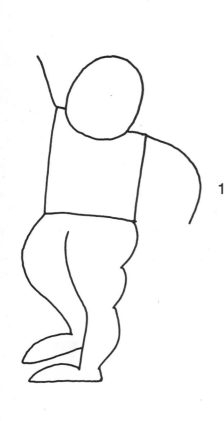

1. Start with this simple outline of the leprechaun. Add the beginnings of his arms.

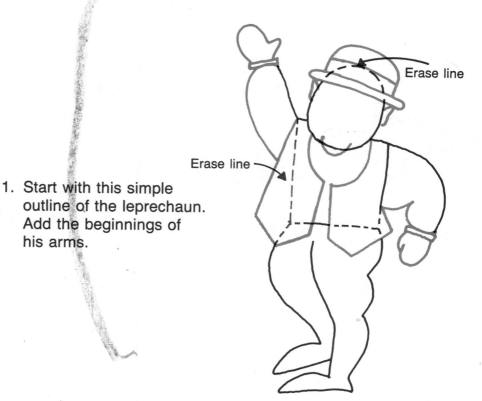

Erase line

Erase line

2. Complete the arms, the hands, and cuffs. Add the hat, ears, double chin, and vest.

Erase line

3. Now fill in the merry elfin face. Add the bow tie, too. Add cuffs to the knickers and buckles on the shoes.

Erase line

4. Add fingers on each hand. Now decorate your leprechaun any way you like.

# The Pot O' Gold

In a folktale, a leprechaun captured in a field said his gold was buried beneath a weed. The man who caught him tied a handkerchief to the weed and ran off to fetch his shovel. When he returned, the leprechaun had tricked him! He'd tied 'kerchiefs around *every* weed.

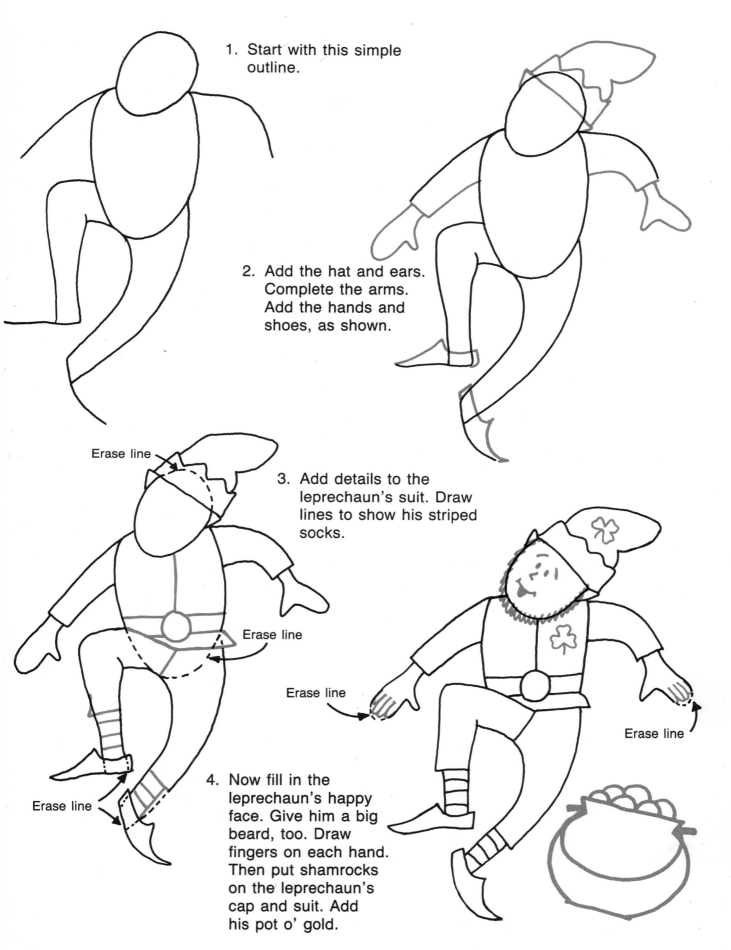

1. Start with this simple outline.

2. Add the hat and ears. Complete the arms. Add the hands and shoes, as shown.

Erase line

3. Add details to the leprechaun's suit. Draw lines to show his striped socks.

Erase line

Erase line

Erase line

Erase line

Erase line

4. Now fill in the leprechaun's happy face. Give him a big beard, too. Draw fingers on each hand. Then put shamrocks on the leprechaun's cap and suit. Add his pot o' gold.

# The Irish Shamrock

Every holiday has its symbol. A heart pierced with an arrow stands for Valentine's Day. A green wreath with a red bow stands for Christmas. A carved jack-o-lantern stands for Halloween. For St. Patrick's Day, it's a *shamrock!* This small three-leaved plant, which looks like clover, is a symbol of Ireland, too.

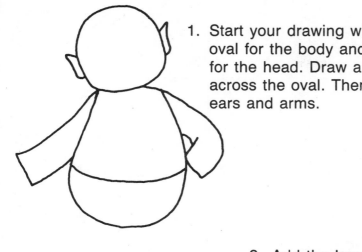

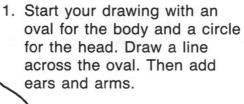

1. Start your drawing with an oval for the body and a circle for the head. Draw a line across the oval. Then add ears and arms.

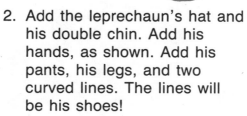

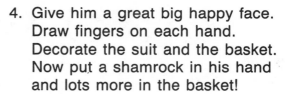

Erase line

Erase line

2. Add the leprechaun's hat and his double chin. Add his hands, as shown. Add his pants, his legs, and two curved lines. The lines will be his shoes!

3. Decorate the hat and shoes. Add a jacket, a shirt, and a collar. Put a basket in his hand. It will soon be filled with shamrocks!

4. Give him a great big happy face. Draw fingers on each hand. Decorate the suit and the basket. Now put a shamrock in his hand and lots more in the basket!

Erase line

Erase line

# The Shillelagh

*Shillelagh* was the name of a famous oak forest that once stood in County Wicklow. Clubs cut from the oaks came to be known as "sprigs of shillelagh." Later, the name was given to any walking stick made of oak.

Erase line

1. Start with four simple shapes to form the head, the upper body, and the arms.

2. Add the *tam,* or cap with a pom-pom. Add the double chin. Then add hands. Add the pants and legs with lines at the bottom for the shoes.

Erase line

3. Add a vest, a collar and tie. Add details to the vest. Complete the shoes. Draw fingers on each hand. Add a big shillelagh in Mr. O'Shaughnessy's hand.

Erase line

Erase line

4. Add a wood grain to the shillelagh. Add stripes to Mr. O'Shaughnessy's socks. Now give him a great big happy face—he's ready for his afternoon stroll!

# The Fairy's Harp

An old Irish legend tells of a harp that is stolen by the god of darkness. So the god of light and the god of art set off to rescue it. With great struggle, they make their way into a cold, dark castle. There, on the wall, is the sacred harp. They seize it and carry it off, bringing it back to the light of day and those who love to hear it!

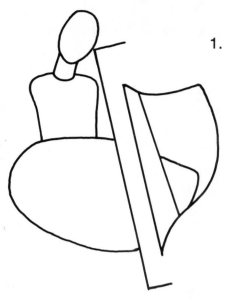

1. Start with these simple lines and shapes.

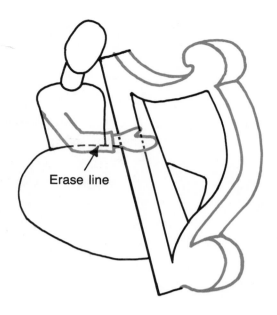

Erase line

2. Fill in the arm and hand. Complete the frame of the harp, as shown.

3. Add the fairy's long, flowing hair. Add her ribbon. Add her collar and cuff. Add her legs and shoes. Then, draw the rock on which she sits.

Erase line

4. Add the fairy's face and wings. Draw the strings inside the frame of the harp. Add shamrocks to the fairy's dress. She's the spirit of St. Patrick's Day. What song would you like her to play?

# Pipers and Fiddlers

Pipers and fiddlers are an important part of St. Patrick's Day celebrations. Fiddlers who know Irish reels and jigs perform at St. Patrick's Day dances. In parades, bands of pipers, some dressed in kilts, march to the wail of bagpipes.

The reed pipe is one of the oldest musical instruments, dating back to the time of St. Patrick. In those days, a simple reed pipe was the main source of music for most people.

1. Start with this simple outline.

2. Draw a piper's hat, then his hands and the outline of the reed pipe. Add his legs and his shoes. Add the lines of his jacket.

Erase line

Erase line

Erase line

3. Fill in the piper's happy face. Draw fingers on each hand. Add details to the pipe and the piper's suit. Don't forget the coat-tails! Give the piper striped socks—now he's ready for the big parade!

1

2

3

# Bodhrans and Bones

The colorful rhythms of St. Patrick's Day come not only from pipes and fiddles, but from flat, goatskin drums called *bodhrans* and the drumsticks that beat them called *bones*.

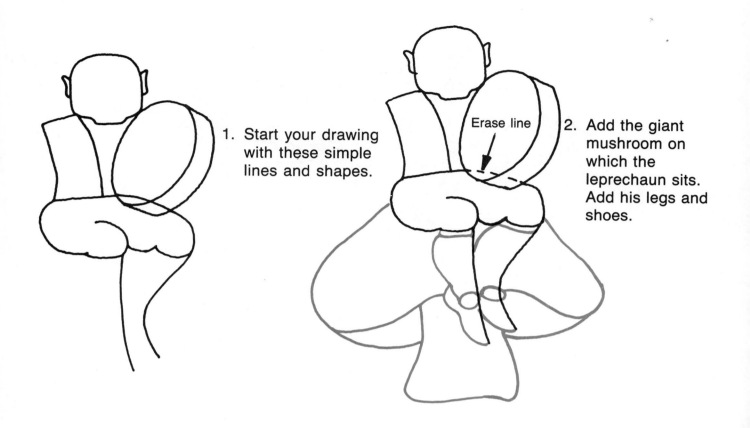

1. Start your drawing with these simple lines and shapes.

Erase line

2. Add the giant mushroom on which the leprechaun sits. Add his legs and shoes.

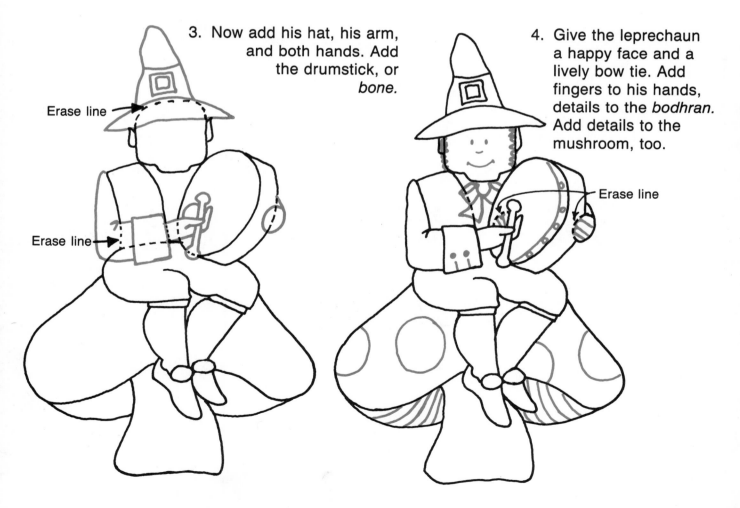

3. Now add his hat, his arm, and both hands. Add the drumstick, or *bone.*

Erase line

Erase line

4. Give the leprechaun a happy face and a lively bow tie. Add fingers to his hands, details to the *bodhran.* Add details to the mushroom, too.

Erase line

# Sweet Molly Malone

In a famous song, a pretty maiden named Molly Malone wheeled her wheelbarrow through the streets of Dublin, crying, "Cockles and mussels, alive, alive, oh!" Molly was a busy street vendor, selling her tasty fish.

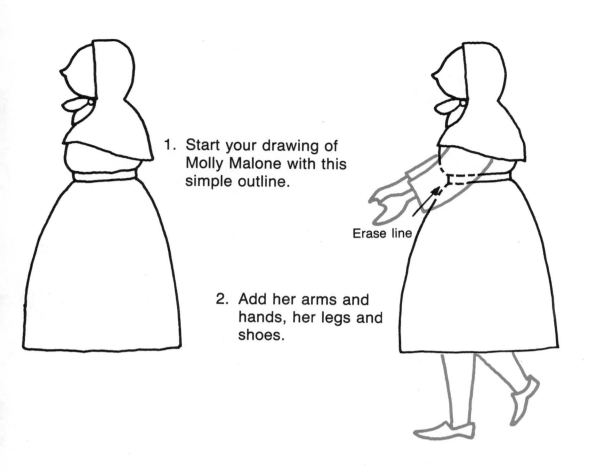

1. Start your drawing of Molly Malone with this simple outline.

2. Add her arms and hands, her legs and shoes.

Erase line

Erase line

3. Fill in Molly's happy face. Add her bright red bangs. Draw her apron. Draw a wheelbarrow, as shown. Add details to the wheel.

# The Irish Jig

As the piper pipes his merry tune,
the leprechauns dance a *jig*.

1. Start your drawing with this simple outline.

2. Add the leprechaun's hat. Then add his hands. Add his legs and pointy shoes.

3. Add the leprechaun's hair, blowing in the breeze as he dances this lively jig. Draw his collar and his belt.

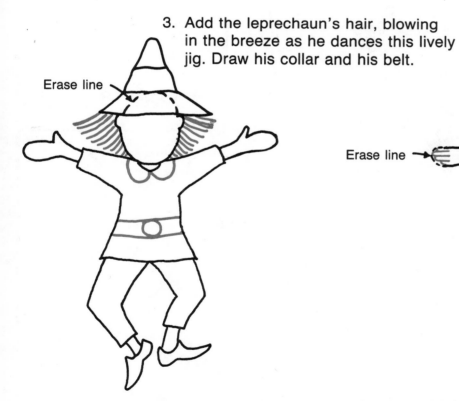

Erase line

Erase line

4. Add shamrocks to his cap and his suit. Draw fingers on each hand. Give the leprechaun a great, big happy face— he's dancing in triple time!

# St. Patrick and the Serpents

Many legends tell how St. Patrick banished snakes from Ireland.

In one legend, he scared the snakes by beating on a drum.

In another legend, he tricked a snake into crawling inside a box. With the snake in the box, St. Patrick sealed the lid and heaved the whole thing into the ocean!

In a third legend, he made the Irish soil so distasteful to serpents that, if they even touched it, they would surely die!

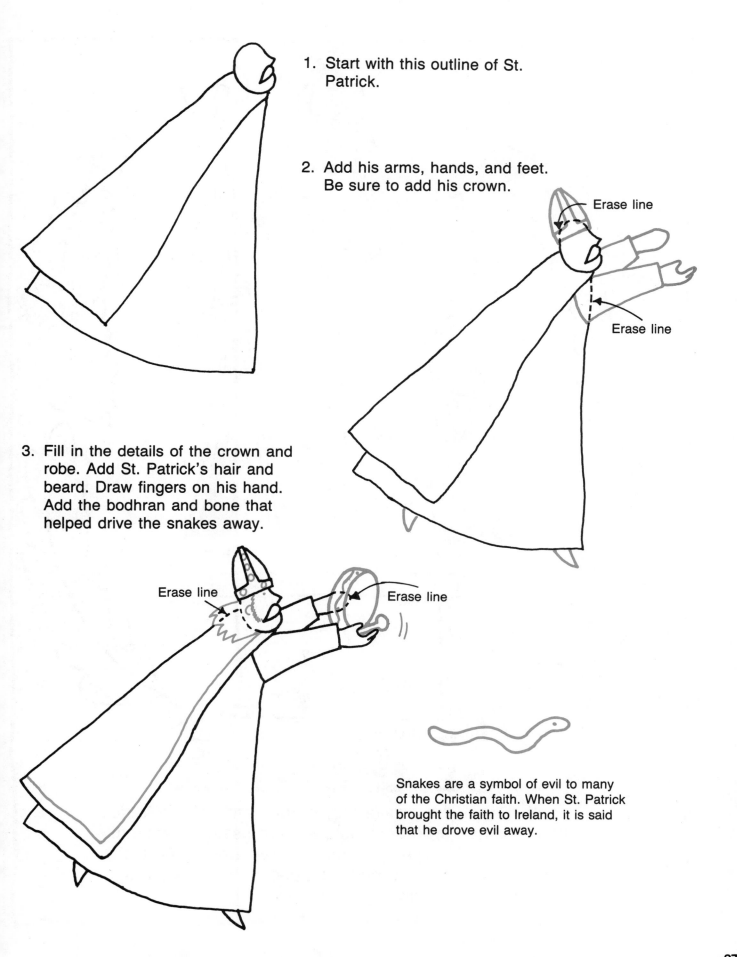

1. Start with this outline of St. Patrick.

2. Add his arms, hands, and feet. Be sure to add his crown.

Erase line

Erase line

3. Fill in the details of the crown and robe. Add St. Patrick's hair and beard. Draw fingers on his hand. Add the bodhran and bone that helped drive the snakes away.

Erase line

Erase line

Snakes are a symbol of evil to many of the Christian faith. When St. Patrick brought the faith to Ireland, it is said that he drove evil away.

# St. Patrick

March 17th is the anniversary of the death of St. Patrick, the missionary who became the patron saint of Ireland. For almost thirty years, Patrick worked among the Irish, building churches and baptizing people. He is said to have died in Armagh in the year 461.

1. Start your drawing with this simple outline.

Erase line

2. Add details to St. Patrick's crown. Add his arms and hands. Draw a large staff, or stick, in one hand.

Erase line

3. Add fingers, then draw a shamrock in St. Patrick's free hand. Add details to his collar. Add the outer robe. Fill in St. Patrick's eyes, ears and nose.

4. Fill in details on the pedestal.

# The St. Patrick's Day Parade

What's that sea of swirling batons, waving pom-poms, pennants, and banners? Some banners bear the names of Irish counties like Kerry and Cork. There are fife-and-drum corps, marching bands, and pipers dressed in kilts. Why, there's even a horse painted green! It must be the St. Patrick's Day parade!

# Happy
# St. Patrick's Day

**The End**